The Days You've Spent

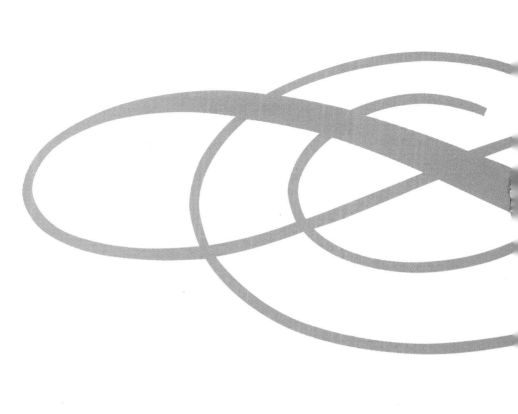

THE DAYS YOU'VE SPENT

poems by suzanne bowness

Tightrope Books

Copyright © Suzanne Bowness, 2010.

ALL RIGHTS RESERVED. No part of this publication may be reproduced, stored in a retrieval system, or transmitted, in any form or by any means, without prior permission of the publisher or, in the case of photocopying or other reprographic copying, a licence from Access Copyright, the Canadian Copyright Licensing Agency. www.accesscopyright.ca, info@accesscopyright.ca

Tightrope Books
602 Markham Street
Toronto, Ontario
Canada M6G 2L8
www.tightropebooks.com

EDITOR: Halli Villegas
COPY EDITOR: Shirarose Wilensky
COVER DESIGN: Karen Correia Da Silva

Produced with the assistance of the Canada Council for the Arts and the Ontario Arts Council.

Printed in Canada.

LIBRARY AND ARCHIVES CANADA CATALOGUING IN PUBLICATION

Bowness, Suzanne, 1976-
The days you've spent / Suzanne Bowness.

Poems.
ISBN 978-1-926639-10-9

1. City and town life—Poetry. I. Title.

PS8603.O97663D39 2010   c811'.6   c2010-900105-2

For my family

Contents

I

Horizons	13

II

At the Boardwalk	21
Asanas	22
Mannequin	23
Missy and the Bad Cats	24
Van Gogh City	26
Potential Still Lives	28
Doppelganger	29
Plant Death	30
Ice Cream Questions	31
Making Time	32
Sofa	33
Nicotania	34
Chocolate Compatibility	35
Fred and Laura Carter	36
Haiku to the Don Valley in Springtime	38
Cooking Lessons	39
The Man from the Seventies	40
Numb	41
Someone Else's Baby	42
Rotting Tomatoes	43

Sinking City	*44*
The Rushed Poem	*46*
Georgina, 92	*47*
Networked Neighbourhood	*48*
Fall	*49*
Cityscape	*50*
Oysters Every Thursday	*51*
Hymn	*52*
I've Never Been to the North Shore of Lake Superior	*53*
Runaway	*54*
Calling in Sad	*55*
Fall #2	*56*
Rosemary	*58*
Sight Lines	*60*
The Gardeners Who Dreamed of Roses	*61*
Summer Morning Routine	*62*
Me	*63*
Last Night in New York	*64*
Here is Where She Feels Most Alone	*65*
Lunch Special F	*66*
Painted Nails	*67*
Shopping at Value Village on a Weekday Afternoon	*68*
Amsterdam to Rotterdam	*69*
Painting a City in Summertime	*71*
Much Resonance Inside	*73*
Hiroshima	*74*
The Morning the Moon Didn't Set	*75*
X: a Body in Motion	*76*
Animal City	*77*
April	*78*
Garbage	*79*

Work Forced	*80*
The Storytellers	*81*
I Heard a Fly Buzz—and I Lived	*83*
Cleaning the Windows	*84*

III

Backward Glances	*87*
Acknowledgements	*93*
About the Author	*95*

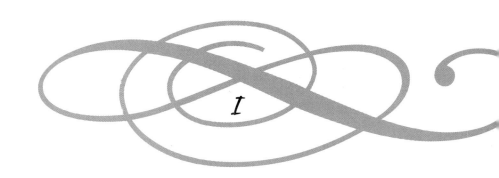

Horizons

1.

Rises from the river flats
    ruptures the fertile ground
        shoots upward

keeper of the valley—

    she

    stretches her concrete trunk
skyward, settles grey arms across trestles,
broad and leaf-like to capture the sun.

Grasps the east and the west   she
    joins one side to the other.
                Horizon
made concrete
    foundation.

Her faithful

    we

stop this fall day
drape our pensive bodies against her solidity
let her bear our full weight
    as we gaze out at yellow and red below

and wonder at the crowding out of youthful green.

Amidst all: she—

is what we wish for ourselves:
constancy, groundedness, strength.

In the spring perhaps we will rejoin her
once more in silent observance
over the changing land:

aspire to be
like she

unjudging

    solid

        still.

2.

Stare
                wide-eyed
                at the great dome.
      Feel   the rush of bodies   here

the cacophony of conversations, the chatter of children,
    the swirl of hellos and goodbyes.

                The last train to Montreal is now departing
                                  departing now.

In the midst of all this: arrival.

I savour the possibilities
of imagined independence.

I see nothing of myself here yet
except for the too-familiar stories
of those who came before me

and not just strangers:
grandparents and parents
their stories blending
with the din.

Alone, I am tempted to borrow
this sense of belonging,
trade neon signs, skyscrapers, and smart cars
for the simpler city they remember—

claim comfort in those snatches of family folklore
strip the city of time.

Instead, I force myself to shake off these false familiarities
leave even the swirl of hellos and goodbyes behind
and step out—

3.

At first, a park is just a park.

> Memories wear in slowly
> > taint casually.

Before it became the site of

> Our First Kiss or
> Her Awful Break-up
> or even That Wretched Downpour

all the park contained was
its essential parkness:
> all trees and grass
> and anonymous children.

The transformations happen elsewhere, too.

Slowly restaurants become
That Bar Where We Celebrated Your Promotion
The Place We Used To Go after Class
> That Place We Avoid
> Because Your Ex Works There.

Even transient spaces become loaded
subway stations taking on
Three Stops 'til Work or
Remember That Dinner Party Way the Heck Out
qualities.

In the beginning, anonymity is everywhere—

slowly replaced
       you miss it
almost.

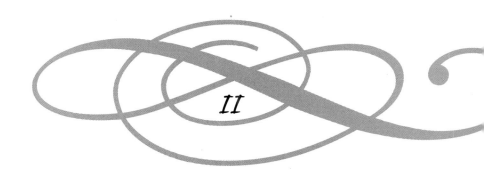

11

At the Boardwalk

The sun settles into the horizon
       a ship drifting gently into harbour.

The tide follows, water flowing
       into the curves of the land.

The sky, almost calm, waits
to be filled with darkness.

Asanas

I am a tree
in a forest
whose foot falters
against my upper thigh
as my mind sways in the breeze.

I am a cat
back curved gently toward the sun

I am a half moon
floating in a dark sky

I am a warrior
strong inside

I am a bridge
between the window
where cars rush by
and the next half hour of quiet.

Mannequin

She is trapped in the store window
but her blank face betrays nothing.

Her captors have arranged her
in a sweetheart negligee
and matching red silk robe—

eternally she carries a champagne glass
—a mimosa perhaps—
to her faceless husband
dressed in Hugo Boss.

He appears ready to leave the tableau for work
but she remains trapped in her lingerie.

Perhaps she will spend the morning
endlessly arranging and rearranging
the oversized metallic paper snowflakes
on the wall behind her.

Missy and the Bad Cats

Deep in sleep, Missy
twitches her lips and paws—
she is being chased
by the Bad Cats again.

Awake she is what I have come to know
as herself
      growly, hissy, jumpy around strangers
      quick to bite even
      the hand that feeds her.

Yet in the innocence of sleep
      her past gives way
                 fear

betrayed in the slight ripple
      of an unseeing eyelid and
            her soft moans.

The Bad Cats are after her again, their damage
      unknowable
           shadows on her happiness.

Even the years don't seem to
take her into their arms,
to allow her a gentle forgetting—
but I will

stroke her little head,
wake her from her terrors.

Van Gogh City

Sometimes when I'm in the mood for arguing

I'll ask you:

> if this city were a painting
> what painting would it be?

Before you can answer

> I jump in with

—*The Starry Night* with all the energy swirling above
raining down in slow measure on the streets—

and you laugh at me, saying,

> don't you know
> that's every city
> not just this one in particular.

No—
this one is *The Potato Eaters*

except the table is in that diner on Queen Street
with the dark booths
where no one speaks above a whisper.

And I laugh at you for being disagreeable
so you say

oh yeah
        well at least I didn't say *Sunflowers*

and we are both

        silent

sipping our coffee
in agreement for a moment

because if there's one thing this city is not
        it's *Sunflowers*.

Potential Still Lives

Outside the art gallery
potential still lives
peek out of mesh bags
as their curators walk them home.

Three plums,
two oranges
(complementary
colours).

A cucumber,
four tomatoes, and
a leafy head of lettuce (tricky).

Butternut squash, assorted gourds,
and a pumpkin (classic).

Each grouping in transit
moves along past potential backgrounds:
the market, a slushy street corner,
the kitchen counter.

At home, potential still lives
are hidden behind the easel, their immortality
dependent on eluding those
who would turn them into dinner.

Doppelganger

Yesterday
in the subway
I saw

a woman who looked more like me
        than me

her hair cut
in my old style.

As she ascended
the escalator
I was walking
        down the stairs.

I wondered about the
cosmic consequences
of eye contact—

how similarly we had lived our lives
the odds of negotiating a trade.

Plant Death

My houseplants conspire against me
while I'm out.

Synchronize their withering
unearth new shades of decay
cultivate exotic rots and moulds
that cause my heart to wilt

knowing that their every demise
causes a small death in me.

I'm a willing participant
in their melodrama.

Singing as I coax
with bigger pots, smaller watering cans,
new fertilizer formulas.

Their triumphant new shoots lift my spirit;
their desiccation crumples it.
Is this cycle their way of marking time—

Or do they sense their power?

Ice Cream Questions

For my parents

Driving through the White Mountains
of New Hampshire
I neglected the scenery
in favour of my storybook friends
    Margaret, Anastasia, Ramona.

To keep our eyes on the road, Mom and Dad
asked my brother and me the ice cream question:

The right answers rewarded with ice cream cones
at the end of the drive.

What is the height of Mount Washington?
Why was it called Lonesome Lake?
What kind of rock is forged by heat?

What kind of traveller
    is forged by the ice cream question?

Years later
our grown-up answers
arrive by postcard.

Making Time

I enjoy too much those few moments
before admitting wakefulness
to give them up.

Today I've hidden under the covers of my bed
an unusual ruse for me
a scratchy voice and a list of excuses.

I've made a whole day here out of a lie
snuggled up with my eyes closed
pleased at what I've gotten away with.

Sofa

> You buy furniture. You tell yourself, this is the last sofa I will ever need in my life. Buy the sofa, then for a couple years you're satisfied that no matter what goes wrong, at least you've got your sofa issue handled.
> —*Fight Club*

I've got my sofa issue handled.

Navy blue, $569 on sale.
Not the cheapest, but definitely discounted,
I tell myself, satisfied.

I never thought I'd go for a sofa
with a tartan ribbing on it,
but what do you know,
one day you're just walking through the Bay
not even thinking about that sofa issue
and there it is—

a bit puffier than I would have wanted,
certainly not as sleek as the sofa of my dreams,
but over the years I've tried those sleeker sofas,
and they're just not as comfortable
for curling up in front of the television.

Who knows, though, how long I'll be able to resist
trading up to a newer model.

Nicotania

Of all the flowers out there
I had to choose a trickster.

Drawn in by your
dreamy summer scent,
delicate in the quiet evening air.

Seduced to breathe you in,
as I sit on the porch
swatting innocent mosquitoes.

Chocolate Compatibility

He scarfs chocolate
in large, carefree bites,
leaving unruly teeth marks
in the middle of each square.

She nibbles chocolate
carefully at the edges
and breaks off a square
to melt on her tongue.

He fills his mouth
so his cheeks are awash
in sweetness, tongue buzzing.

She centres the taste on her tongue
whittling the same piece down
savouring bit by bit.

He kisses her suddenly
hard on the mouth
sweetness overflowing
as he pulls her toward him.

She takes his hand and laughs,
puts the rest of her chocolate
in her pocket, so they have some for later.

Fred and Laura Carter

For Fred

Fred and Laura Carter lived in a little house that Laura sometimes wished was painted yellow like buttercups but in fact had black shingles and a Stop sign at the corner of the lawn where all the neighbourhood kids could spin around the pole and fall down dizzy.

With a crabapple tree at the side, swans swimming in the gardens out front, a big birdbath at the back, and a deck that Fred and Laura could practise jumping off, often daring to clear the red rosebush with its treacherous thorns, the yard was full of adventure despite the fact that it did not have an inground pool like the house behind, or even an above-ground pool like the house two doors over.

Inside the house was a big yellow kitchen with a large table where Fred and Laura sometimes coloured with crayons, although more often they would colour in the room with the shaggy blue carpet. Fred and Laura sometimes kept a store, but not every day, and when the store was in business Laura liked to be in charge. Fred sometimes ran a garage with many cars. But most often they had to go to work outside the house with awkward leather briefcases and hair that was parted by a mysterious grizzled stylist who would wait in the anteroom near the front door. They called this room the vestibule and its windows had criss-crossed black strips that matched the colour of the roof of the house and looked prettiest when powdery snow had drifted into the corners.

Fred liked to dress in women's clothing on occasion. Fred and Laura were lucky to have an appropriately large stage at the end of a long winding staircase in front of which to perform. Perhaps it was because Fred was shorter than Laura, although that too would change, that he would often claim ownership of the distinctly female wig. Fred frequently stole the show, but Laura didn't mind, partly because he was indeed the better performer and partly because she sometimes felt bad that he was often the recipient of her hand-me-downs. But occasionally he pulled her hair and those instances kept her from ever feeling too sorry for him. One time they held a festival to celebrate socks and really gave it their all. Socks are really quite under-celebrated, and their time had come.

Laura and Fred sometimes ate supper at a small table, with smaller chairs, that looked particularly small when you compared it to the big table in the yellow kitchen. Later, Laura would try to remember when they stopped using the small chairs, and in forgetting she felt wistful, the same way she would years later when she saw the concrete swans again, a little worse for wear but still swimming in the front gardens.

Haiku to the Don Valley in Springtime

whose idea, this
    springtime breathing so green through
our own Valley floor

Cooking Lessons

Sweetness can be found in unexpected places—
the curious case of the caramelized onion,
the intimacy of a shared recipe.

Along with garlic and ginger, the onions
have this way of flooding the kitchen
with a jumble of savoury scents.

He described it
as the promise of what's to come.

She chops the carrots in tiny strips,
—*julienne* was his word—
with practice she is almost as fast.

Peppers and mushrooms sautéed together,
a swirl of colour, a flick of her wrist—
dangerously they soar above the pan.

A flourish of parsley, but a rough chop of thyme,
and before things were complete—

Looking down at the table
she realizes

she's taken two plates down
from the cupboard by mistake.

The Man from the Seventies

The man from the Seventies
isn't just here to be seen
and couldn't care less
what you think of his old-school haircut.

The man from the Seventies
is here to be edified, like the rest of us
and carries his slim portfolio with thin fingers,
tucked under the sleeve of his beige trench coat.

The man from the Seventies
is at the free concert on Friday and the lecture on Sunday.
He hangs back but looks on, intent,
his solitude noticeable but his presence all-knowing.

Numb

Imagine nearly 2.5 million people living in this city
(that's just the core, not the 5.5 million in the GTA).
And presume that everyone goes to the dentist
every six months (not everyone does, but play along).
And almost nobody goes to the dentist on weekends,
so that's 261 days for everyone to go.

So dividing 2.5 million by 261 leaves 9,579 people
going to the dentist every day.
Except that most go every six months
so that's in fact double at 19,157 every day.

Now imagine that half the adults going
will have to get some cavity work done once a year
(half is arbitrary, I haven't looked into this statistic
further than my own dental hygiene experience,
which is admittedly a poor record to rely on).

But if you've made it this far, imagine
the number of people every day

walking around with frozen smiles,
numb.

The Days You've Spent | 41

Someone Else's Baby

At 3 p.m. on a Sunday afternoon
she holds someone else's baby.

Listens to his soft cooing,
a life in her protective arms;
she imagines his first words
whispered like a secret,
but not to her.

Rotting Tomatoes

Rotting
tomatoes are
causing anxiety
dissolving into their basket
rotting

Ripe at
the beginning
of the week, five bodies
each sagging and sinking into
one form

Growing
a clean white mould
delicate like whipped cream
and hard to deem a colour of
decay

Frozen
by my own odd
fascination with their
impending demise, I keep them
watching

Their end,
their ominous
falling, their slow dissolve
under the menacing pressures—

Sinking City

Who knew that
beauty and time
could be so conspiratorial?

La Serenissima,
you sink despite
their shrewd efforts

a crumbling city
in a beautiful lagoon.

At last I've made it
here to witness for myself
your loveliness laid out
before me.

I too
am caught in time,
hours passing as I
wander the cobbles

trace your mosaics,
peer through the windows
of your churches.

Now here, I half regret that I've seen
you're real, and
already I plan my return,
knowing
you may not wait for me
to come again.

The Rushed Poem

This poem must be written
in the ten minutes
between shower and breakfast.

Ten naked minutes
only a robe
to stop the steamy shower warmth
fading from the skin.

Only a blank notebook
to stop the half-remembered dreams and waking thoughts
from fading into deadlines, appointments, and to-do lists.

Books of poetry by the bed flipped through like pornography,
anything for a shortcut to image, metaphor—

before the day rolls in,
before the notebook is abandoned.

Georgina, 92

For my friend

I'd only ever known you old
but your stories held the proof of your youth
a life distilled in moments—

the one where you stood in your slip while the Air Force girls
swirled around you, piecing together a uniform so you could
make a New York City debut, represent your corps in style

the time Laura found the mouse in the kitchen,
ran shrieking from the house until you disposed of it

the time Billie, then pint-sized, suggested
that he liked the singing on the radio better than yours

the time
you had to hop a ride to Hamilton
to prove you'd be
the best cashier
for a new store opening
      and the manager's words repeated—

    Georgina, you catch that train and don't you miss it.

Networked Neighbourhood

Everyone knows everyone in a caring sharing town
don't meet her at the laundromat
word gets around

she'll meet you in the city
three or four years down
cause everyone knows everyone
in a caring sharing town.

Fall

Perhaps it is the gentle wind
    smooth on the fine hairs of our arms.

Or that the colours seem particularly
    exact.

Perhaps it is the smell in the air
                 rich
in its tumble of
reminders

    of fallow seasons, of lovely decay,
    increasing clarity, and impending

        snowfall.

Perhaps it is those things that create
a sharpness so immediate
    no words are needed.

Perhaps that is why we have fallen
into brief silence
    in front of the   perfectly
        yellow tree.

Cityscape

Concrete landscape
majestic in its peaks
of too-tall towers
with rivers of
cars streaming through.

People who chat
in outdoor cafés
or wait to
cross the street
look like
tufts of wild growth
from this height

sprouting up
amidst the
grey.

Oysters Every Thursday

The man holds out his hand
beside the stencilled sign
Oysters Every Thursday.

I try to understand
why still they wait to dine
as the man holds out his hand.

Judging from the demand, it's
surely a feast divine
with Oysters Every Thursday.

But all seems so unplanned
the margins undefined, as
the man holds out his hand.

And though the crowd expands
the message has lost its shine
Oysters Every Thursday.

So while he still must stand
I will not join the line
where the man holds out his hand
for Oysters Every Thursday.

Hymn

She sits amidst the carols
and God swirls around her

in the words of each hymn
she looks to find God and
sometimes does, the notes
rising from her throat

finding strength in
harmony.

I've Never Been to the North Shore of Lake Superior

Upon gazing at a print of Lawren Harris's North Shore, Lake Superior (1926), *hanging on my wall for many years*

I've never been to the North Shore of Lake Superior
but when I go I know I'll find
radiating turquoises and yellows.

I know I'll close my eyes
feel buttery sunshine on my face
draw white crispness
like air into my lungs.

When I open my eyes I know
my gaze will fixate on a lone tree
      climbing toward a sky that gets lighter
         as it approaches the apex
where the sun's beams radiate.

A sky where clouds move in
but never quite take over
and the sun's glow

      accents the clouds in a way
      that feels strangely familiar.

Runaway

Wrapped in the colours of this night
she is deep inside herself now.

Thoughts like running water
rush through her mind.

Looking for answers in the shadows
she keeps time with the swift click

of her stilettos on the pavement
as they pace the fading light.

Calling in Sad

Despite stern instructions
her body refused to get out of bed that morning.

Lucky her arm was more responsible
and reached for the telephone—

fingers dialling
lips articulating

the appropriate words
for that inappropriate state.

What excuses do you make
for that other part of you that sometimes sickens

that part without
blood vessels to blue the skin
or mucus to rattle the rib cage?

Fall #2

You tell me that describing
    something beyond words is
especially challenging.

For instance, the gentle wind
    smooth on the fine hairs of one's arms.

You tell me that colours, even when particularly
    exact in the autumn light,
        can seem   abstract
            on the page.

So I am at a loss

    silenced first by those smells of coming winter

    so rich that they evoked
        antique memories

        of fallow seasons, of lovely decay,
of increased clarity and impending snowfall.

Silenced again—you're right—by the limitations
that cause us to

fall

into brief silence
at the thought of the
perfectly
yellow tree.

Rosemary

Rosemary dances around the garden,
her needles weaving through the air
like sheer scarves, waving
against a backdrop of stolid potato shoots
and utilitarian squash runners.

She knows the comparison is backwards—sheer scarves
are only a pale imitation of her.

She has both looks and grace
scent and taste
and she knows it, shows it—
rosemary is the opposite of oblivious
she is nocent
flaunting, drawing everyone in—

What kind of herb is that? they ask.
Oh *that's* Rosemary.

Meanwhile, others in the garden try to compete—
asparagus wave their lacy fans;
stately corn, staunch like soldiers,
if unable to control their tassels floating in the wind;

peas storm the lattice with their tendrils
grasping and twirling;
beets hint at a ruddy underside
with their leaves, again something special but
nothing like rosemary, who dances on—

Other plants may be getting their roots in a twist over her
but why should that be her problem?

Sight Lines

Standing in front of her on the streetcar this afternoon
a young woman tired beyond her years
watches the old couple haul their buggy
on board, struggling with their many bundles.

Oblivious to her own charms, she stares
at their bulging bag of apples and jugs of juice
as if each represents the fruits of their love
rather than a simple trip to the shops.

So hungry for their secret, so anxious
to learn their longevity, she stares the old woman
up and down, looking for clues, missing

the young man farther back
who tries to catch her eye.

The Gardeners Who Dreamed of Roses

A beautiful vision, it was—
with radiant red blooms and dainty white ones.

All thorny, as it turned out.

Roses with names like Bourbon Queen
Deep Secret, Strawberry Ice, and Burning Sky.

The gardeners who dreamed of roses
imagined a parade of admirers
through their garden,
lingering longest
near the most brilliant blooms
as they brushed at the air to waft the fragrances
and compliments around.

The gardeners who dreamed of roses
dreamed someday they'd have a garden party,
with a violinist and fancy dresses,
serve canapés and ice wine.

Yet despite their careful mixes, sand, peat moss, and
buckets of water, the gardeners efforts
only reduced the stalks to dry sticks.

By season two they'd adopted a careful use
of the word "dormant"
to describe the reticent bushes.

Summer Morning Routine

Across the street
the two hanging baskets
sway in the morning breeze,
a greeting of pink geraniums.

The curly-haired man
and his matching golden retriever
have come back early
from their walk

and the skinny redhead
is already ferrying
her huge green travel mug
and too-full backpack to work.

The blue car leaves,
then the red one—
the little blond twins
are wearing white today.

Those whiny cats
are yowling again in the alleyway

and it won't be long before
a chorus of lawnmowers
starts humming
its summertime tune.

Me

I am one line on a page in the middle of a book.

Last Night in New York

We've become familiar too quickly,
just as I have to leave.

Corner shop with the only copy of the *Times* left
late on Sunday; I snap it up and head home,
flight to catch in the morning.

My suitcase bulges
with these inadequate souvenirs:
books from the East Village,
theatre stubs pressed between their pages.

I no longer jump at the shadows
or hesitate to walk a dozen city blocks
just to see where they will lead.

Tonight my bag is packed—and I should be getting to sleep
but I'm sitting on a too-high loft bed,
listening to jazz I'd never put on at home.

Here is Where She Feels Most Alone

Here is where she feels most alone.
Sick at the doctor's office by herself after work.

Conspicuously alone amongst the other snifflers
hand unheld, feeling foolish
even at the thought of calling
somebody to her side.

Nobody at her side a few weeks later
the evening gapes free
dinner at the little café she loves
still warm in her stomach.

Spontaneously she decides to walk a little farther—
who cares if fat snowflakes melt in her hair against
the energized darkness of shadowy streets.

Here is where she feels most alone.

Lunch Special F

Lunch special F please
I don't even bother to
Look at the menu

Today is a day
For miso soup with tofu
City girl comfort

Coloured lanterns float
Above me freely, they sway
Mingling with muzak

Today is a day
To read my novel alone
At the lunch table

Wait for that very
Reliable perfection
To arrive at last

Six little pieces
      ebi, kani, maguro
Precise on my plate

Painted Nails

We who paint our nails
know that it's hard to pull off
while maintaining the sense
that you're more
        than just painted nails.

People see painted nails
and assume you're not
the kind of person
who can dig a garden
take care of children
watch foreign films.

They wonder about your other
frivolous habits—

categorize, judge,
lament, project, extrapolate, condemn,
forsake.

Of course, I only paint my nails
in sheer, respectable colours
(not like the scarlet-taloned receptionists at work).

Shopping at Value Village on a Weekday Afternoon

For my shopping buddy

We're playing hooky from life
    on a weekday afternoon and once again

your enthusiasm for antique tin
and vintage everything

    distracts you
so I can walk speedily
to the back
where someone
has been donating
some really current novels
to the book bin lately.

When I return
with my smug bargains
    and an offhand suggestion
for you to check out my leavings

you are polite enough
not to call me
on my underhandedness,

pulling instead a sweater
you thought might suit me
from your overflowing shopping cart.

Amsterdam to Rotterdam

If you fall asleep on the train
between Amsterdam and Rotterdam,
slumber overcoming you
like an armed bandit,
overstuffed backpack beside you
with its closest strap wrapped
around your shoulder
in the last action your tired mind
could take post-jetlag
before giving up on safety,

rest assured that when you wake
you will be watched by
a disapproving middle-aged lady
whose face you will no longer remember
five years down the road
(or even by the time you make it to Berlin)
but whose scolding you'll remember
long after you've forgotten
even the countryside scenery whizzing by,
a scolding seemingly detailed but almost
indecipherable in its noble but broken English
(better than your non-existent Dutch)
no doubt outlining the folly
of your lapsed vigilance and the dangers
that can result, a scolding that will have you

taken aback at first but that you will grow more
and more grateful for as the years pass

and will cause you, in turn,
to look out on future trains for those
who look as tired as you felt,
so you can reciprocate this guardianship.

Painting a City in Summertime

To paint a city in summertime,
nestle it above the trees
of a lush green park—

make it a cloudless day, or maybe
allow one cloud
to reflect in the glass
of the tallest office tower.

Let the grey of the buildings
pick up a little of the green of the park,
and vice versa.

Be gentle with the smog,
forgive the actual day just slightly.

Let a kite drift playfully into the air,
allow it to float a little higher than it would in real life.

Don't forget the teenagers
throwing their Frisbee between them,
their surliness temporarily
abandoned beneath the tree
with their summer school book bags.

Put time and detail into the lovers
strolling hand in hand.
Capture her blush.

Loosen a tie or two on the cluster of businesspeople
who stride quickly toward their meeting.
Have one stop and shade his eyes
as he looks toward his building.

Paint a bunch of anonymous children running
through the park in small groups of two or three,
along with the back of the soft-shouldered middle-aged woman
on a wooden bench in a grey suit watching it all.
Make the sandwich she's unwrapped
on the bench beside her seem extra tasty.

Let the office towers extending to the sky
be mirrored by tree trunks that dig deep into the ground,
giving the city roots.

Much Resonance Inside

> *We can complain because rose bushes have thorns,*
> *or rejoice because thorn bushes have roses.*
> —Quotation taped at eye level inside a Toronto MRI machine

She lies quietly in the white coffin
and tries to imagine herself away.

Magnets click around her and she wonders
about the one who taped the quote above her

about that person she feels alternately
kinship and hostility.

Hiroshima

Political education begins
in the impossible
number of cranes, dripping
like tears from the stone angel's face.

The Morning the Moon Didn't Set

On the morning the moon didn't set
she and he
walked hand in hand
under the twice-bright sky.

The moon's luminous whiteness
matched the sun
as they looked around
for another sign the world was ending.

Finding none they sat down
    together
on a bench in the leafy park.

On the morning the moon didn't set, she
could sense that everything changed   except
that nothing had changed—

her hand still in his
their world still making sense

perhaps even more so as they gazed
at sun and moon, reunited at last.

X: a Body in Motion

She dances with precision—
choreographed mathematics
    a body in motion.

Left hip swings out in fixed trajectory—
taut belly delicately exposed
    a fraction of an inch.

Time slows down
as the hip curves back
    against a heavy bass beat.

Yet it is the variable that is key—
lush hair swinging wildly around her face
    a dangerous inconstant.

Animal City

The man who drives the bus
is slowly turning into a rhinoceros.

At first I thought it was just
his neck getting thicker
his cheeks jowlier
but now that his skin is thickening
into a tough grey hide
it's really starting to show.

The woman who sits
in the front row of the bus
would normally be the first
to point this out
but her fingers no longer point as well
now that they're turning into talons.

Outside the man watering the flowers
is beginning to develop a bit of webbing
between his toes
and the lady at the bank
can't say more than a few words
without emitting something of a whinny.

I'll be okay though—
I've always thought I'd look good with
a larger wingspan.

April

April wallows in her own
breathtaking abilities.

High on herself
she pulls us into
her extravagance.

We are complicit
as we allow ourselves
      to get lost in her greenery
her flowering apple blossoms
her springtime excess.

Her exit is appropriately dramatic too
as she lets each small flower tumble away
into delicate pink clouds.

Garbage

Garbage day and the lawns are a wasteland—
    old metal strewn across the grass like bones;
refrigerators whose usefulness spanned
entire childhoods, now lie with broken phones,
bent tire rims, rusted toasters, ripped cushions.
Frail byproducts of our restricted time,
    signs we too should grant ourselves permission
to make room for new things, and leave behind
resentments, old naïve expectations.
Burn up mental trash, watch its ashes fly
away, so we no longer feel temptation
ever again to trundle it back inside.

Even the fiercest grudges can't live on
when tied up and placed curbside on the lawn.

Work Forced

Down this street
her younger self
weaves ghostlike
through the crowd.

She is new to this
9-to-5 world, she is
learning its shortcuts:

how to blend in,
how to dodge careening cars
and unhurried old ladies on the sidewalk,
the most efficient spot to stand
       on the subway platform,
when to grab the morning paper
and where to discard it   she's learned

to push to get ahead, but not too much
—quicker to move with the crowd
       than against it.

The Storytellers

Nobody calls anybody
but everybody shows up,
like family.

The room is dark,
details painted over with a thick brush,
smoke hanging in the air,
masking expectation.

Slowly, the room grows loud with recognition,
eyes and ears adjust
to reveal familiar faces, voices
reconnecting: not where are you working but
what are you working on.

In time a hush signals the divide—
as pilgrim reader journeys forward
and seasoned listeners fade back;
silence grows tangible.

Outside, these subjects
would be too big, conspicuous,
you'd have to apologize before you started.

Inside, everyone here knows
the way that silence breaks—
chest expanding, lips dry,
as words rip into air,
exposed thoughts like raw knuckles,

as you hold on
and wish back the silence.

Speaking other people's thoughts,
whispering in borrowed voices,
the room fills with our stories.
Parched listeners, we
greedily consume these details,
watering our imaginations until we too are
swimming in shadows and colours.

Listening, you fall into yourself,
gather your own light and darknesses,
become spirited like a child
allowed to stay up late.

Later, we'll spill out into the night, satiated,
not knowing when the next time will be
but sensing it was time to go.

Like family, we listen
and always come back.

I Heard a Fly Buzz—and I Lived

I heard a fly buzz—and I lived
Now what? In spite of that he buzzes, the Stillness in the Room
disrupted by the slice of his wing through morning air
Between the Heaves of my half-slumbered body—

My eyes dart like his body around the room,
My breath growing strong to the day,
Mind onset for battle to rid the room of this King.

I will myself out of bed, body still resisting the day
Yet that portion of me assignable to this task
determined in its

Uncertain stumbling between sleep and wake,
I flail with slipper in hand then pause at the morning
calm and beautiful outside.

Open the window and release—

Cleaning the Windows

Not until she saw the bright sun streaming
one late quiet afternoon last weekend
did she notice how filthy the windows
were, how she'd been living under a cloud
of dust, of fine obscurity now made
plain by the sharp glare of late autumn light.

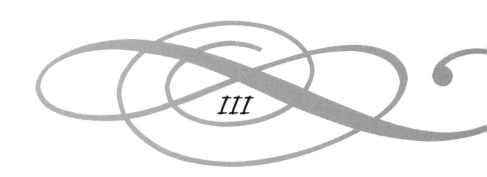

Backward Glances

1.

Look, they've knocked down
that brick building
near the university
where we sat sometimes
    at night
    and talked
about the way things would someday be—

Remember that one time
    you put your hand
        on my shoulder
and knew just when to ask
what was wrong.
That other time when I pulled you to your feet
and reassured you

that a long walk
could do wonders.

2.

Far from this sunny October afternoon
    we'll rendezvous, my friend,
at this big rock on Cumberland street
and all will be revealed.

We'll sip our drinks, the expensive lattes of our later years.

Relive this warm glow
    of late fall sunshine on our arms
    of the dreams
        we dreamed today.

Then, as now, our eyes will be closed, warmed
    as we let the sun seep through our eyelids,
remembering the girls we were.

3.

Taking the streetcar
along St. Clair
I push the window open
      to feel the wind again
through my hair
reminds me of speed cycling
through Toronto streets

dodging doors
      potholes
           glances

locking up and taking the subway
if I was late or
taking a chance
      and sailing
past Sam's, Eaton's, Lichtman's
everything whirling by
all the way
down Yonge.

4.

This city swallows me
a casual predator.

Bound by its grid of avenues and streets
I wonder at its trappings—

I used to wonder how long I could stay here
I used to think I would leave.

Now I know the day arrives
when you just wake up

willing prey, ensnared in the days you've spent.

Acknowledgements

Thanks to my parents Bill and Sandra Bowness for their support, for providing lots of books around the house, childhood trips to the library, and for never questioning (much) my decision to make my living as writer.

And to my year-and-a-half-younger brother Bobby, who will always be Fred Carter.

Thanks to the following journals that published poems in earlier versions: the *Literary Review of Canada* ("Van Gogh City") and *Pagitica* ("Calling in Sad").

Special thanks to everyone I've met in various literary groups and writing circles over the years, from the Hart House Library Committee to the Taddle Creek Writing Workshop to Moosemeat, and especially to writing teachers like the encouraging Bruce Meyer and writing friends, like Sylwia Przezdziecki who knows what it is to write before the day rolls in.

Thanks to Steven Heighton for looking over the almost-finished manuscript when he was writer-in-residence at the English Department at the University of Ottawa and complicating poems like the one about the yellow tree. Thanks, of course, to everyone at Tightrope Books for helping to sharpen this collection into finer form, particularly the cheerful Shirarose Wilensky.

Finally, thanks especially to my longstanding writing and shopping buddy Halli Villegas, who is now my editor and poetry publisher as well. I look forward to hanging out and writing with you for many years to come. Are you in a cage?

About the Author

Suzanne (Sue) Bowness is a writer and editor. Born in Montreal to parents who had fled a more conservative Toronto in the 1970's, she returned to attend the University of Toronto and, by the end of her first ten years in the city, ended up living just blocks away from where her paternal grandparents had settled on the Danforth. After starting a career in magazines as online editor for the late weekly *Saturday Night* magazine, Sue turned to freelance writing and editing, which she has pursued for the past eight years, writing for such publications as the *Globe and Mail*, *National Post*, *University Affairs*, *Profit*, *Poets&Writers*, and many others. Her poetry has been published in the *Hart House Review*, *Trinity University Review*, *Pagitica*, *Qwerty*, and the *Literary Review of Canada*. Her play, *The Reading Circle*, won first place in the 2006 Ottawa Little Theatre's National One-Act Playwriting Competition. After writing an MA thesis at York University on the founding and early years of *Saturday Night* magazine, she is now pursuing a PhD in English at the University of Ottawa where her dissertation continues to investigate nineteenth-century Canadian magazines. She is currently working on a short story collection, a screenplay, and a novel. Her website is www.codeword.ca.

FOR the LOVE of POETRY

www.TightropeBooks.com